From La Fayette to D-Day

Two Centuries of French-American Friendship

éditions
italiques

Every man has two countries, his own, and France.
Thomas Jefferson

Two nations do not exist who are more unified by the ties of history and mutual friendship than the people of France and the people of the United States of America.
Franklin D. Roosevelt

I have two loves : my country and Paris.
Josephine Baker

America is my country and Paris is my home town.
Gertrude Stein

Published by Éditions Italiques s.a.r.l.,
55, rue de Grenelle, 75007, Paris
Tel.: (1) 42.22.59.57 - Fax: (1) 42.22.59.61

© Édition Italiques, Paris, MCMXCIV
Published under the direction of Jean-Pierre Turbergue
Text : Philippe Conrad, Jean-Pierre Turbergue
English Adaptation : Thomas Crampton
Revision : Lynn Weiss
Artistic Director : Gérard Gagnepain
Iconography : Jean-Pierre Gillet, Jean-Noël Lallement
Layout : Alain Postel
Proof-reader : Marie-Claire Tossut
Production : BDI
Printed in France by IME, 25110 Baume-les-Dames

Distribution Ouest-France
Dépôt légal 2ᵉ trimestre 1994
ISBN 2-910536-01-7

une 6, 1944, Dawn

G.I.s of the first and fourth divisions of the US infantry leave their landing ...ts and begin the long walk to the shores of the beaches code-named Utah and ...ha. The final assault on Hitler's "Fortress Europe" has begun. America, once again, has come to the call of France.

Following a long night during which 1,200 planes of the Royal Air Force continuously bombed the northern coast of Normandy, the weary German defenders awoke to see an incredible enemy armada — thousands of battleships of all types and sizes anchored offshore at positions that had been carefully reconnoitered by spy submarines.

The invasion force stretched almost 100 miles from Cotentin to the mouth of the Seine. The fleet was so dense that, as one eyewitness later put it, "you could have walked all the way from the Isle of Wight to the French coast."

At 05 : 30, when the flotilla opened fire, the horizon was suddenly ablaze. The biggest naval bombardment in history had begun. The air was alive with shells fired from the great battleships. The noise was deafening.

"We were attacked by an unimaginable number of boats and planes," recalls a German corporal, "one after the other, our bunkers were hit by shots from enemy guns aimed with great precision because of the reconnaissance planes circling over our positions. The sky was literally black with Marauders, Typhoons, Liberators, Flying Fortresses and Mustangs. There was no sign of our planes. As for the anti-aircraft artillery, there was complete silence except for the occasional shot of the 20 mm guns."

In the name of Liberty

The sea is rough, and the tide is rising. Tossed about in the landing craft, deafened by the noise of explosions the American 1st and 4th division infantries move in on their respective targets : two beaches separated by the mouth of river Douve, code-named Utah and Omaha. These names would forever be written in blood and burnt into the long, collective memoir of Franco-American friendship.

One hundred and sixty years earlier, Rochambeau had come to North America, bearing arms to aid in the Thirteen Colonies' fight for independence. American soldiers now came to La Fayette's homeland to return the precious gift of liberty. ∎

General Pershing declared the famous "La Fayette, nous voilà" (La Fayette, we are here) as American troops came to the aid of France in 1917 ; it could easily have served again as the motto for the soldiers who came ashore at Utah and Omaha beaches... In 1944, it took 5,339 warships to liberate occupied France. In 1781, Admiral de Grasse had only needed 24 warships to break the British fleet's control of the Chesapeake Bay. This victory proved a turning point in the Colonies's fight for independence.

When they called New York Angoulesme

The love story between France and America began well before the colonists called their country the United States. As early as the XVIth century, French explorers returned to the coasts of the New World which they had hoped to make New France.

"Though the natives are extremely odd and covered with variously colored feathers, the physical attributes of the countryside are most pleasant. Situated in the middle of precipitous hills is a wide and deep bay. It is easily large enough to accommodate a good sized sailing vessel..."

This entry, dated April 1524, describes the one day port of New York City. The steep hills will be called Brooklyn and Staten Island, and a bridge, named after the narrator will connect the two : Giovanni da Verrazano. Born into a rich Italian family of Lyons, France, Verrazano was a Frenchman at heart. Jean de Verrazane, as he was called in his adopted country, had sailed from Brittany three months earlier in search of the mythical "North-West passage" to India. After a stopover in Madeira, he and the crew of the *Dauphine* saw the New World on March 7, 1524. They were off the coast of present-day North Carolina. Fearful of the Spanish in Florida, he looped back to explore the North. Crossing the immense bay between Cape Hatteras and the coast of Virginia, Verrazano thought he had seen the Eastern Sea, leading to the Pacific, and called it the Isthmus of Verrazano. This name, which later appeared on maps of the New World, was to encourage many false hopes. The Indians were very friendly to the travellers, and the French affectionately called present day Maryland "Acadia" (the Indians' kindness did not stop the French sailors from taking a native boy back to Europe as a souvenir). Sailing by day, and mooring at night, the *Dauphine* continued north off the coast of Delaware and New Jersey.

On April 17, Verrazano lay claim to Manhattan in the name of Francis I. He wrote the French King, "Sire, we called this land Angoulesme, the name you once had when lesser in fortune... As for the beautiful bay that is formed in this land, we gave it the name of Sainte-Marguerite, in honor of the princess, your sister, who is above all women in virtue and in spirit." ■

The French in Florida

Sixty years before the Mayflower pilgrims landed at Plymouth Rock, French Huguenots, also fleeing religious intolerance in Europe, set up a colony in Florida. These brave colonists might have played an important role in the foundation of the French États-Unis, *but history decided otherwise.*

When Admiral de Coligny suggested sending Protestants to live in Florida to practise their religion in peace, the French king, Charles IX jumped at the idea. He saw an opportunity to counter the ambitions of Catholic Spain in the country described by Franciscan Marcos de Niza as a "new Eldorado." Jean Ribault, a Huguenot from the coastal town Dieppe, was chosen to lead the expedition. The ship weighed anchor in February 1562, and by April 30, she reached what they called Cap des Français, in present day South Carolina. On May 1st, they had their first contact with the apparently peaceful natives. A French column, emblazoned with the royal fleur-de-lys soon stood next to the small colony on the bank of the May River (now called St. John's River). It marked the French claim to the land they considered "the most beautiful, rich, and pleasant in the world."

Having established a colony at the mouth of the Port Royal river, (on what is now Parris Island, South Carolina) Ribault left thirty soldiers to build a camp called "Charlesfort," in honor of the king, while he returned to France for re-enforcements and supplies.

The religious wars prevented his immediate return. When a second expedition, led by René de Laudonnière, finally arrived in Florida in June 1564, famine and mutiny had overcome Charlesfort. A second colony, Fort Caroline, was established on the May River. Its fate was even worse. Men deserted to take up piracy, relations with the Indians degraded, and famine threatened. The survivors were relieved to see seven masts on the horizon. Jean Ribault had finally kept his promise. He landed on August 28, 1565 with 600 colonists. The joy was short-

1562 : The French took possession of Florida by erecting a large column, bearing the arms of their king, on the banks of the May River.

lived. A storm sank the boats. Those who escaped death at sea were killed by the Spanish, who were only too happy to finish off the "Lutheran Filibusters." On September 20, the troops of Pedro Menédez de Avilés massacred the garrison in a surprise attack. This bloody encounter put an end to French colonial ambition in Florida. ∎

Louis XIV, King of Louisiana

April 9, 1682 on the banks of the Mississippi River. Robert Cavelier de La Salle, outfitted in full dress uniform, sword in hand, read a proclamation that gave his king "the country Louisiana." One hundred and fifty years after Jacques Cartier, Cavelier de La Salle offered France another chance to carve out an empire in the New World.

Born in Rouen, Normandy, in 1643, Robert Cavelier de La Salle was one of the greatest explorers of the North American continent. The son of wealthy parents who settled in Montreal in 1666, he could easily have led the life of a rich colonist. Gripped by the stories told him by the Indians, he swore to be the first to open the passage to the Great Western Ocean towards China. Pushed by the Governor General and supported by Jean-Baptiste Colbert, advisor to the King, and by King Louis XIV himself, Cavelier de La Salle made numerous expeditions to the Great Lakes and into present-day Illinois and Ohio. He left behind him a magnificent network of forts. After several fruitless attempts, the indefatigable traveller left Saint Louis (south of Lake Erie, in the territory of the Miami Indians) with twenty Frenchmen and thirty scouts from the Mohican and Abénaquis tribes to find the Mississippi River. When they reached the river on February 6, 1682, the ice was too thick to break. After a week, the ice began to break up, allowing the expedition

to descend the river by canoe. Leaving behind places visited years before by Joliet and Marquette, they entered the territory of the Arkansas Indians, then went on to the Natchez, who gave them a very warm welcome. The two tribes were at war with one another, so the expedition didn't pause for too long. The river became wider. Soon the vegetation grew more exotic, and they sighted alligators. On the fifth of April they noticed that the water was briny. The following day, they reached the fork of the Mississippi Delta, and soon the area where the river swept into the sea. Several days later they erected a cross below which was placed a plaque that read: "In the name of Louis XIV, King of France and of Navarre, April 9, 1682." After they had chanted *Vexilla Regis* for the king, and a triumphal Te Deum, several shots were fired in salute. Cavelier de La Salle then read, in the presence of a public notary brought on the trip for this purpose, the proclamation giving Louis XIV "the country of Louisiana and all the seas, ports, provinces, all the peoples, nations, cities, villages, and mines of this country, as well as the length of the river Colbert or Mississippi, and all rivers that empty into it from their springs to the Gulf of Mexico." The proclamations were received several months later by Louis XIV. The "Sun King" was so pleased to gain such a vast territory that he named Cavelier de La Salle Governor and

Leaving France in 1684, Cavelier de la Salle's second expedition overshot the Mississippi Delta, and never found Louisiana again.

gave him four ships and 200 men to begin colonization. The flotilla left in July 1684. While the voyage to the Gulf of Mexico was without incident, the expedition by-passed the Mississippi Delta, and ended up farther West, in Galveston Bay. The region was inhospitable, and the conditions in which the foundation of the future Saint Louis of Texas took place were very bad. Famine and mutiny soon threatened. On March 19, 1687, Cavelier de La Salle was killed by his own troops. Not long afterwards the settlement was overrun by Indians. The dreams of the explorer from Normandy ended in tragedy. ■

A Brotherhood of Arms

French-American friendship, formalized by the treaty of February 6, 1778, was sealed in the blood spilled on the battlefields of Virginia and Yorktown.

The court of Versailles followed closely the events leading up to the American Revolution. When, in 1776, the Thirteen Colonies proclaimed their independance, Vergennes, the Foreign Affairs Secretary, saw a perfect opportunity to take revenge on Britain, and thus advised the King to support the rebels. Fearing a war with the British, Turgot, the Minister of Finance, was less enthusiastic. King Louis XVI was not inclined to assist a rebellion which undermined another monarch. Despite popular opinion in favor of the Revolutionaries, France's support was far from certain when Benjamin Franklin arrived in Paris on December 27, 1776. He joined Silas Deane as American Minister to France. Deane was a wealthy Connecticut businessman, who, chosen in haste, had produced no concrete results. Franklin's reputation as a man of great learning, who lived modestly, greatly pleased the

Court. Franklin soon had French support for the Revolutionary cause. Official aid was at first discreet. But the number of volunteers offering to help the Revolutionaries grew rapidly. There was a great deal to draw young Frenchmen to America : the attraction of new ideas, a thirst to fight their hereditary British enemy, a desire for adventure and the chance for exotic travel in the New World. Several months later, Silas Deane wrote, "the rage to sign up to serve with the Americans is continually growing. As a consequence I am inundated with offers, many from persons of consequential rank..." The King himself had to intervene when members of distinguished families wanted to leave for the New World. The count of Noailles and the count of Ségur, two of the most important names in the French kingdom, wanted to leave with the young Marquis de La Fayette. It was feared that these

Benj. Franklin

young men would compromise the neutral position of France. Noailles and Ségur bowed to the pressure, but La Fayette stole onto the boat *La Victoire* which sailed first to Bordeaux, then to Spain, and finally on to Georgetown, where he arrived in June 1777.

Many of the volunteers were greatly disappointed in the New World. Most of them did not speak English and they did not understand how the Revolutionary Army, unlike anything in Europe, could function on a battlefield. Furthermore, their social background made it difficult for them to adapt to the democratic style of George Washington's soldiers. Welcomed with great enthusiasm in Philadelphia, La Fayette even

offered to serve in the army as a foot soldier, and to pay his own way. Franklin, however, explained to the Continental Congress that it would be politically advantageous to enlist foreign soldiers whose families could influence the court at Versailles. La Fayette was finally appointed to the rank of General. Returning to the front just as the English General Howe marched on Philidelphia, he was injured at the battle of Brandywine. Soon after, he followed Washington to his headquarters at Valley Forge. The winter of 1777-1778 was a particularly tough one. Badly clothed, badly nourished and badly armed, Washington's army was on the verge of collapse. At this point, an attack by the English would almost certainly have changed the course of the war. In Paris, Franklin did his best to convince the court to adopt the American cause officially through a formal alliance with the United States.

Opposite : Louis XVI (above) ; Benjamin Franklin is received at Court (below).
Right : signed on February 6, 1778, the French-American Treaty of Friendship is the oldest official document recognizing the U.S.A.

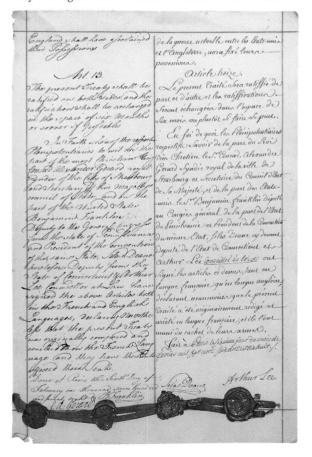

13

Charles Vergennes

Charles Gravier, count of Vergennes, was born in Dijon, Burgundy, in 1719. His uncle, the reknowned diplomat Chavigny, taught him the complexities of foreign affairs. In 1750 Louis XV named Vergennes the Minister to the Elector of Trèves. In 1754, he was appointed ambassador to the Sublime Porte in Constantinople. There he established himself as the principal French diplomat for Affairs in the Middle East. Criticized at court for having married a woman below his social stature, Vergennes lost his position in 1768. He was called back to diplomatic service by Broglie, head of Louis XVI 's secret diplomacy corps, after four years of forced retirement. He was later appointed ambassador to Sweden.

In 1774, he became Minister of Foreign Affairs, a position he occupied until his death in 1787. Careful to "contain within reasonable bounds domination of the British," as he wrote in a report on December 8, 1774, Vergennes became the principal French supporter of the American Revolutionaries.

Closely observed by the British ambassador, Lord Stormont, Vergennes remained reserved. He wanted to be certain of Spanish support before taking a stand. The surrender of General Burgoyne at Saratoga in November 1777, tilted the scales in favor of the Revolutionaries. Vergennes feared that the Americans would settle for a disadvantageous peace with Britain. So on December 17th, he informed Franklin that Louis XVI had decided to recognize the independence of the United States.

The French to the rescue

The resulting Treaty of Commerce and Friendship was signed on February 6, 1778. The Revolutionaries' situation was such that the French could have made any demand in the treaty, taking advantage of the vulnerable United States. Instead the French policy looked far into the future. Vergennes wrote to his ambassador in London on March 17, 1778: "We did not want to procure any commercial favors that might make other nations jealous, such that the United States might one day accuse us of taking advantage of them." One week later he stated, "The authorized American deputies were open to giving us any exclusive rights of trade we might have demanded. We were aware of that. But through the recognition of the United States as a member of the family of nations, the King wanted to create a bond that would serve posterity and be as solid and enduring as is possible in human affairs." The French policy prompted Benjamin Franklin, a great student of human nature, to say, "The truth is that this nation loves glory and loves to protect the oppressed."

Back on the battlefields of North America, the British began to realize that time was against them. After taking Philiidelphia they prepared themselves to deliver the death blow to the Revolutionaries. They wanted to quickly exploit tensions within the Revolutionary ranks, notably the rivalry between Washington and Gates, the victor of the battle of Saratoga. General Clinton took command of the British troops after

Howe's resignation. Fearing a French blockade of the Delaware and an attack on the city by the Continental Army, Clinton moved towards New York.

Washington followed behind and launched an attack at Monmouth — an audacious military manœuvre that would have been a decisive victory if Charles Lee, the commander of the vanguard, had not inexplicably disobeyed orders and retreated from ground he had captured and held. Court martialled, Lee, accused by some of treason, was finally released. The error had been commited. Washington was forced to stop his offensive, and instead set up headquarters in New Brunswick while Clinton went on to New York.

Arriving in July 1778, the French fleet under Admiral d'Estaing came to the aid of the Revolutionaries, for the first time in force. A siege was planned ; Estaing would move in by sea, while the American General Sullivan would arrive by land to take Newport, Rhode Island. Unfortunately a violent storm arose, putting

Above: *An eighteenth century 'political cartoon' by Buffon, representing "England begging one hundred times a day, while externally calm, but suffering from interior turmoil" (Voltaire). Spain and France shake hands in the background, oblivious to the spectacle.*

Opposite: *A map of the American positions, held by the Generals La Fayette and Sullivan, the day after the retreat from Rhode Island on August 30, 1778. It wasn't until the French expeditionary force arrived, under the command of Rochambeau, that the tide turned definitively in favor of the Continental Armies.*

an end to this first attempt at military cooperation between the new allies. Estaing headed south to the West Indies for the winter. This setback did not bode well for the Americans. Paris would not look kindly on a failed military operation ; but the Revolutionaries were very much in need of assistance and re-enforcements. At the end of 1778, La Fayette obtained permission from the Continental Congress to go to Versailles. He was well received, and knew how to

Pierre de Beaumarchais

Pierre Augustin de Beaumarchais, a man of letters and an adventurer was born in Paris in 1732. The son of a clock-maker, Beaumarchais was introduced into society by the banker Paris-Duverney. Knighted by the King at age 29, Beaumarchais became famous for his plays *The Barber of Seville*, and later *The Marriage of Figaro*. Mozart based two operas on these comedies. For several years, Beaumarchais conducted secret missions for the Count of Vergennes, the King's Secretary of State and a great champion of American independence. In December of 1775, Beaumarchais wrote to Louis XVI to request money for the American Revolutionaries. For two years, more than three million pounds were discreetly passed on to Hortalès & Compagnie, a front company created to filter money to the Americans. The Spanish, happy to support those fighting the British, also gave a million pounds. The money, used to buy guns and ammunition, was delivered to the Continental Congress in the beginning of 1777. Because of his involvement in another arms smuggling affair, Beaumarchais was exiled at the start of the French revolution. He didn't return to France until 1796, where he died three years later.

convince Vergennes and Maurepas to throw the weight of France into the battle. Among the plans that had been envisaged was a large-scale landing in Britain. Ships had been prepared for this purpose. The project never saw the light of day. But the fleet gathered in Saint Malo and Le Havre made it technically possible to send an expeditionary force to the New World as La Fayette requested. Louis XVI was still worried about dissent among the Revolutionaries and feared that Spain's Charles III, although allied with France against England, would dislike too decisive an American victory next door to his overseas empire. Still, France eventually sent to General Washington 5,000 men chosen from their best troops. La Fayette was too young to command the expeditionary force. He was sent back to America to announce the imminent arrival of the long-awaited re-enforcements under the command of Rochambeau.

America, we are here !

Leaving Brest, the convoy sighted land at Newport, Rhode Island, on July 11, 1780. Among the officers, were some of the most important names in France : Montmorency, Custine, Chartres, Noailles, Lauzun... The hopes raised by the arrival of the French were short-lived : soon after, a large British fleet was sighted. It was under the command of Admirals Arbuthnot and Rodney. It spoiled the plans for a quick attack on New York. The Hartford meeting, organized by La Fayette between Rochambeau and Washington, resulted in another request for more French re-enforcements. Only a full-sized naval force could save the situation. To make matters worse, when Washington returned to his camp at West Point, he learned of Benedict Arnold's treason. One of the Colonies' most brilliant military minds had gone over to the enemy. Becoming chief counsellor to General Clinton, Arnold pushed for quick action to exploit the weakness of the Continental Army. Victims of the naval blockade, the American soldiers were neither paid, nor fed, nor clothed. Rochambeau began to worry,

Marie-Joseph de La Fayette

Born in 1757 at Chavaniac, in the Auvergne, Marie Joseph Paul Motier, Marquis de La Fayette, joined the King's army at the age of fifteen. After only a year he received an officer's commision. Married to the daughter of the Duke of Ayen, a member of the powerful de Noailles family, La Fayette had many important connections. He met Benjamin Franklin who soon rallied him to the American cause. In April 1777, disobeying the King's orders, the young Marquis left for North America, where he commited himself to the service of the Continental Congress declaring, "It is in the hour of danger that I wish to share your fortune." Without any real military experience, and despite his letters of recommendation, he was rejected several times before being accepted as a Major in the Revolutionary Army. Soon after he had been injured at the battle of Brandywine, in September 1777, La Fayette was given command of a division. In 1778 he made a trip to Europe which lasted several months. When he returned to the revolutionary fray he had obtained a promise from Louis XVI for a French expeditionary force to help the Americans. After the siege of Yorktown and Cornwallis' surrender, La Fayette returned to France, and in 1782 was made full Marshal. A leader among the liberal aristocrats, a deputy of the Auvergne, an abolitionist and a Freemason, he considered himself the "hero of liberty in two worlds," a French Washington. At first in favor of the French Revolution, he was named commander of the National Guard in July 1789, and later commander of the Northern armies. As an advocate of an enlightened monarchy, La Fayette deserted the French Revolutionary cause in 1792, following the arrest of the Royal Family. Interned by the Austrians, he was set free in 1797 and returned to France where he stayed out of public life during the Consulate and Empire periods. A deputy under the Restoration, he returned to the United States in 1824 with his son, Georges Washington de La Fayette. Throughout his stay, which lasted more than a year, he was greeted as a returning hero. La Fayette visited more than 182 towns and left the country rich in memories, gifts (36,000 acres of land in Florida) and silver. These were just rewards for a man who had freely given a good part of his fortune and his life to support the noble cause of American inde pendence. La Fayette died in Paris in 1834.

17

George Washington

Born in 1732, to a wealthy family of Virginia plantation owners, George Washington had, ironically, begun his career as a soldier fighting those who, twenty years later, would become his greatest allies. In 1754, as a young Lieutenant-Colonel in the Anglo-American forces, the future first president of the United States fought the French during the skirmishes that preceded the Seven Years War.

On May 10, 1775, he was named commander-in-chief of the Continental Army. He wasted no time transforming a group of volunteers into an effective fighting force. Aided by military advisors from Europe — some reproached his favoritism towards La Fayette — Washington put together an army that took the offensive, even after that dreadful winter at Valley Forge, and routed the English before finally defeating them at Yorktown.

quite legitimately, about the effectiveness of these "men pushed to the limits of their resources." Once more Louis XVI and Vergennes responded to the needs of the Revolutionaries. On May 16, 1781, despite the terrible state of French finances, the ship *La Concorde* brought six million pounds to Washington. The American General wanted to attack New York. Rochambeau, however, thought it more prudent to head south, where the English General Cornwallis had not yet managed to win a decisive victory against the American fighter Greene, who used guerilla tactics. Clinton ordered Cornwallis to keep a minimal force in Yorktown, on the Chesapeake Bay, where they had the support of the Navy ; he would then send the remaining troops to reinforce the garrison in New York, where they thought the major battle would

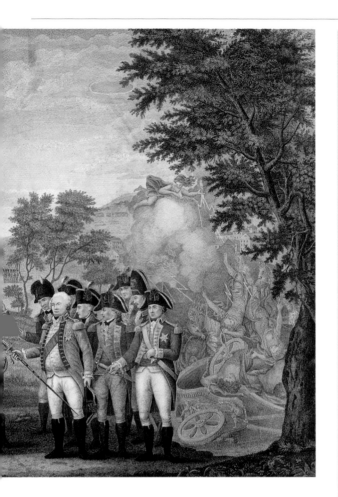

François Joseph de Grasse

François Joseph Paul, the count de Grasse, was born in Provence, in the South of France in September of 1722. In 1738, he started sailing on galleys belonging to the order of Malta. He began serving France in 1740 ; he fought in the War of Succession in Austria and in the Seven Years War, after which he became captain of a warship. He left for America in 1778. The commander of a squadron the following year, he played a glorious role in the battle of Dominique in 1780 and in the capture of Tobago in 1781. Promoted to commander of the Atlantic fleet, he defeated the English Admiral Graves on September 5, 1781 during a decisive battle in the Chesapeake Bay, which led to the American victory at Yorktown. The following year, fate conspired against him. While planning to seize Jamaica with the Spanish, he found himself face to face with the English fleet commanded by Admiral Rodney. Fighting against superior forces, de Grasse's battle lines broke. He was forced, after almost eight hours of combat, to lower his flag and surrender his ship, *The City of Paris*. Taken back to London as a prisoner, he was liberated in August 1782, when relations between France and England improved. While he was disgraced and snubbed at court, a war council acquitted him of any offense. He died in Paris January 14, 1788. To honor his memory, the French Navy launched a cruiser in 1938 bearing his name.

Above : *the surrender of Yorktown.*
Below : *September 5, 1781. A decisive naval victory in the Chesapeake Bay.*

take place. Cornwallis was thus left vulnerable and Washington, knowing that de Grasse's fleet was enroute, was readily convinced to attack Yorktown. Moreover, de Grasse, who was sailing back to the continent after a series of victories in the West Indies, had sent a message to George Washington, telling him that he preferred fighting in the Chesapeake Bay because it was deeper than the Hudson River, and allowed for greater manœuvrability.

On August 19th, crossing New Jersey, the Franco-American troops headed toward Virginia. On August 30th, Washington and Rochambeau triumphantly entered Philadelphia. From there they marched c Yorktown with an army of 18,000 men. There wei 9,000 Americans and 5,000 French to which wei added 3,300 more when the Marquis de Saint Simc arrived from Saint-Domingue with de Grasse's flee Cornered with a mere 7,000 Redcoats, Cornwallis w in a desperate situation. Hope appeared on Septemb 5th, when 22 ships were sighted on the horizon. Th fleet, commanded by Admiral Graves, had left Ne York two days earlier to rescue Yorktown. The tic seemed to be turning against the Revolutionaries, b de Grasse saved the day. In the Bay, the French shij

were sitting ducks. De Grasse manœuvered brilliantly ; he slipped his fleet around Cape Henry and set up in formation around the *Ville de Paris*, the largest vessel of that period. When the battle began in the open seas, the English had already lost.

When the canons stopped, one British ship had sunk and five more were seriously damaged. No French ships were destroyed and only two were damaged. Graves retreated ; the French victory was complete. Cornwallis had counted on the naval re-enforcements to back him up so he hadn't bothered to protect his positions. On September 28th, the Revolutionaries deployed their forces : the French on the left next to the Americans ; followed by La Fayette's Franco-American corps ; General Washington's troops ; and finally the troops under the command of Prussian General von Steuben (who had fought with the Revolutionaries since 1777). The fate of the British was sealed. On October 17th, the anniversary of the surrender of Burgoyne at Saratoga, the Star Spangled Banner flew over Yorktown. The defeated British garrison marched between two rows of the victors — the French on the left, the Americans on the right. The officer representing Cornwallis, who claimed to be ill, wanted to surrender his sword to Rochambeau. But the French General, gestured toward Washington, who respectfully refused the sword. The fall of Yorktown, which had been their stronghold, forced the British to negociate. The Treaty of Versailles, signed September 3, 1783, ended the American War of Independence. The official birth certificate of a new nation, this treaty was also a symbol of the friendship between France and the United States. It was a friendship for which the two countries would time and again pay for with their lives. ∎

Left : Cornwallis surrenders his sword to General Rochambeau at Yorktown. Thousands of copies of such engravings based on paintings, were sold in the XVIII th century. They helped popularize French-American friendship all over the world.

Jean Baptiste Rochambeau

Jean Baptiste Donatien de Vimeur, comte de Rochambeau, was born in Vendome, south west of Paris, in 1725. His first combat experience was in 1742 during the Austrian War of Succession ; he participated in the Bohemian, Bavarian, and Rhine campaigns. After which he was named advisor to the Duke of Orléans.

He distinguished himself again during the German campaign of 1757-1758, and was appointed to the rank of Marshall in 1761.

When France sided with the Revolutionaries, Louis XVI and his minister Vergennes, wanted to limit their support to providing more naval assistance. But by the end of 1779, the situation in the colonies had became so difficult that the King agreed to give La Fayette 5,500 men. The soldiers had been chosen from among the best regiments in the kingdom. They were placed under the command of Rochambeau whose own son had joined the expeditionary force.

They sailed for America in July 1780. Rochambeau advised Washington to attack Cornwallis in the South instead of Clinton in New York. This decision led to the victory of Yorktown.

When he returned to France, Rochambeau became military governor of Picardy, in Northern France. Although he was a noble, he rallied to the cry of the French Revolution, and assumed command of the Northern Armies in 1790.

He resigned from his post in 1792, following a disagreement with General Dumouriez. Arrested during the Terror, he was released by Napoléon and received a Marshall's pension in 1803. He died in Thoré in 1807.

France Sells Louisiana to the United States

December 20, 1803. The French tricolor flag which had long flown over New Orleans had come down. The Stars and Stripes now flew in its place. Louisiana had been sold to the United States for 80 million francs.

In 1763, Louis XV abandoned to Spain, the vast Mississippi territory that Cavelier de La Salle had claimed for Louis XIV a century earlier. The secret treaty of San Ildefonso, signed in 1800, which gave Louisiana and Florida back to the French, worried the newly elected president, Thomas Jefferson : Napoléon Bonaparte's presence on the Mississippi meant the threat of a French colonial empire in North America. But war with France at that point would have required an alliance with the British, which was then unimaginable. Jefferson preferred a diplomatic solution. In March of 1803, James Monroe rushed to Paris to negotiate. In the French capital, he received an unexpected welcome : the Premier Consul knew that France would

The star spangled banner replacing the French tricolor in Louisiana.

soon be at war with Britain and he did not want to run the risk of another enemy front. So he authorized Talleyrand, the Minister of Foreign Affairs, who had visited the United States, to sell Florida and Louisiana for 100 million francs.

Sensing the urgency of the French negotiators, Monroe tried to reduce the price. On May 2, 1803, they decided on the sum of 80 million francs. Congress ratified this agreement October 20th, despite Republican opposition. The Republicans were appalled because Congress had not been consulted sooner ; they worried about granting automatic American citizenship to the people of the new territories.

The treaty was advantageous to the New Republic because it doubled its size. It was also a boon for Napoléon, who hailed this "ceding of land which will affirm forever the power of the United States [and give] England a naval rival who, sooner or later, will best them." Monsieur de Laussat, the prefect of Louisiana addressed the population : "Prudence and humanity together with a larger political perspective have given a new direction to France's benevolent intentions for Louisiana : she has given the territory to the United States of America. Dear Louisianans, you have thus become the token of the friendship that cannot fail to grow stronger between the two Republics." American possession of Louisiana took place on December 20, 1803. The French flag was lowered and the American flag was hoisted amidst great fanfare. There were four toasts during the banquet that followed : with Madeira wine, they toasted the United States and Thomas Jefferson ; with Malaga wine, they toasted Charles IV of Spain ; and with champagne they toasted the French Republic and Napoléon Bonaparte. The fourth toast called for the eternal happiness for the newly acquired territory of Louisiana. ■

American Nature Revealed

After the War of Independence, exploration of the vast virgin western territories began in earnest. No one contributed more to the discovery of the New World's wildlife than the naturalist Jean-Jacques (John James) Audubon.

Born in Saint-Domingue on April 26, 1785, Jean-Jacques Audubon was the illegitimate son of a wealthy French planter and a Creole woman — a fact he tried to conceal all his life. A former naval officer, who had fought in the battle at Yorktown, Audubon's father took his son to France when he returned. The boy was just four years old when he arrived in Nantes, Brittany. But his artistic ability earned him an apprenticeship with the painter Jacques-Louis David. Audubon went to Pennsylvania in 1803, where his father owned land. There, he discovered the sumptuous flora and fauna of North America. From that moment on, his life was dominated by three passions : hunting, painting and ornithology. In 1808, he married an American. He would dedicate almost 40 years of his life to exploring, notebook in hand, the vast wilderness of his new country — Kentucky, the valleys of the Mississippi and Ohio, Florida, Louisiana and Texas. In 1833, he visited the Labrador coast, the habitat of numerous water birds. In 1842, he traversed vast areas of Canada. The following year he left Saint Louis to go up the Missouri as far as Montana. Audubon's monumental work, *The Birds of America,* was published in London in four volumes between 1827-1838. It received a triumphant reception in both the New World and the Old. Audubon was welcomed into the prestigious Academy of Science in Paris.

The famous naturalist lost his vision in 1846. He died in New York in 1851, aged 66. In the United States today, the Audubon Society for the protection of Nature, perpetuates the memory of this great artist who was one of the most illustrious Frenchmen from America. ■

Jean Laffitte

Consider the incredible journey of this famous pirate of French origin, who helped the Americans win the "Second War of Independence" against Britain. Lafitte also helped sponsor the publication of Karl Marx's Communist Manifesto.

Born in 1781, in what was then the French island of Saint-Domingue, Jean Laffitte plundered the seas around the West Indies in the early years of the nineteenth century. Daring to the point of recklessness, he once anchored in New Orleans with ships, scarcely disguised, that he had just captured. The following year, in 1805, he established himself in that great Louisiana port town and accumulated a large fortune selling "ebony."

In 1807, Laffitte set up a base in Barataria, back on the bayous of the Mississippi. It was sheltered from rough seas and enemy ships, but within reasonable distance to slave and other markets.

In 1812, Laffitte and his brother Pierre were arrested. Released with just a warning, the pirates resumed their activities with renewed vigor. The brothers were investigated again, but their band members killed several inspectors, and managed to bribe the rest. The impunity with which they operated created such an outrage, that Pierre Laffitte was arrested again in June, 1814. At this point the English, once more at war with the United States, contacted Jean and offered him the rank of captain and a warship if he joined their side. Struck by a previously well-hidden patriotism, the pirate went to New Orleans to negotiate the release of his brother; in exchange he agreed to fight with the Americans. Despite their misgivings, the local authorities, expecting an imminent attack from the British, accepted. Thanks to the intervention of Laffitte and his brigands — suddenly transformed into "courageous gentlemen" — in January of 1815, the scales were tipped in favor of General Jackson against Pelkenham's Redcoats. Pardoned by President Madison, Laffitte disappeared soon afterwards. He went to Europe where he met Karl Marx; sympathetic to his ideas, he helped finance the publication of his works. Laffitte died anonymously in 1854 in Illinois. ■

OLD ABSINTHE HOUSE, NEW ORLEANS QUARTERS OF THE PIRATE LAFFITE IN 1807

Laffitte's adventures as recounted by Hollywood : Yul Brynner playing the role of the famous pirate turned patriot.

Charles Alexis de Tocqueville

Innovative and pragmatic, the political institutions of the young American nation attracted the brightest minds of Europe. Among them was a French legal expert whose penetrating analyses remain relevant today.

Charles Alexis Clérel, the Count of Tocqueville, was born in 1805. His career as a Justice Magistrate began in 1827 at Versailles. In 1831, he was sent to the United States to investigate its penal system. There he studied the institutions and ways of life in the new nation. Tocqueville published his observations as *Democracy in America*, between 1835 and 1840. It enjoyed immediate success in France as well as in England (Tocqueville married and practiced law in England).

The acuity of its analyses and its almost clairvoyant commentary, made *Democracy in America* an immediate classic. To this day, it remains an extremely accurate study of the American political system. Tocqueville was one of the first political thinkers to point out the potential danger of the "dictatorship of the majority" inherent in a democracy. He also insisted on the importance of an independent press and judiciary.

Elected to the prestigious *Académie Française*, he was a liberal member of the opposition to the government, and deputy from the Manche region of northern France. As such, he defended the freedom of education and free trade.

After the 1848 Revolution, he was elected to the Assembly and charged with drawing up the constitution of France's Second Republic. Many aspects of this constitution bear his trademark and were clearly inspired by the American example. In particular, it calls for presidential elections by universal suffrage every four years and the separation of the powers of government. As deputy at the Legislative Assembly of 1849, and Minister of Foreign Affairs, de Tocqueville opposed Napoléon III's coup. He went into exile first to Italy and then to Germany. In 1859, he died in Cannes in the south of France. ∎

The texts of the "Founding Fathers" greatly inspired French political thinkers of the mid-nineteenth century.

La Fayette against La Fayette

Having fought faithfully on the battlefields of Virginia and Yorktown, eighty years later, many Frenchmen chose to side with either the Yankees or the Confederates in the American Civil War.

An imperial declaration of June 10, 1861 forbade "all French citizens living in France or abroad, from joining the armed forces or engaging as mercenaries with either one of the belligerents." Still, between 1861-1865, nearly 25,000 of Napoleon III's subjects took part in the bloody American Civil War. Polignac, the son of one of Charles X's ministers and a general in the Confederate army, won the battle of Mansfield in Louisiana. For this victory he was known as the "La Fayette of the South". In the meantime, New York's 55th regiment was composed

> *Many Frenchmen took part in the American Civil War, including two Princes who fought alongside the Yankees.*

of French volunteers under the command of the Count of Trobriand. They were known as the "Gardes La Fayette." An aristocrat from Brittany, Régis de Trobriand earned the rank of Major General in the American Army, a feat only one other Frenchman had ever achieved before : the Marquis de La Fayette.

Trobriand was appointed colonel in 1867, and he took command of the 51st infantry regiment which was stationed in the Dakotas. After two years of fighting that hostile environment and the Sioux Indians, he was promoted to the rank of General. He was charged with eliminating the Montana Indians, who attacked and robbed settlers and thereby interfered with Westward expansion. Appointed military commander of Utah in 1870, Trobriand smoothed tensions between the Mormons and the Federal Government. After a short stay in Wyoming, he assumed his final post in Louisiana, where he retired. He died there in July of 1897 at the age of 81. After his death, his daughters published two memoirs entitled : *Four Years of Campaigning with the Potomac Army*, and *Military Adventures in the Dakotas.* ■

When Liberty Lit the World

The Statue of Liberty, which has welcomed immigrants since 1886, is one of the greatest symbols of the United States. On an island in New York Harbor, Lady Liberty stands as the most enduring emblem of French-American friendship.

October 28, 1886. 10,000 official guests, and an enthusiastic nation await the inauguration of the statue "Liberty Lighting the World." The statue, erected on Bedloe's Island at the entrance to New York Harbor, commemorated France's role in the American Revolution. Congress allocated funds for the event provided that "not one dollar be spent on spirits or tobacco." Fortunately, private enterprise easily met that demand, and the crowds were able to smoke or drink as much as they wished. When the statue was unveiled, revealing the unparalleled dimensions of the monument — 46 meters high from its base to its top and weighing 200,000 kilograms, it was the biggest monument of its type ever constructed — the American applause could be heard across the Atlantic. The sculptor, 52 year old Frédéric August Bartholdi, was known in the United States for his statue of La Fayette. Bartholdi had given America this statue ten years before. In France, he was better known for his colossal Belfort Lion — a gigantic figure sculpted in red sandstone that symbolized the heroic resistance of Alsace during the 1870 war with Prussia.

The Statue of Liberty under construction in MM. Gayet-Gauthier's foundry on rue de Chazelles in Paris in 1884.

Built in France in sections, the Statue of Liberty is made of copper supported by an iron skeleton constructed by Gustave Eiffel, architect of the famous tower. Its 300 separate pieces were molded and shaped in Paris, and then reassembled in New York Harbor. The statue rests on a granite pedestal 25 meters high.

Money for the statue itself came from a generous subscription fund in France and its pedestal was financed by the United States. ■

The First Artistic Exchanges

In the second half of the XIXth century, American Artists "invaded Paris as though it were the far West." Among them were many fairly distinguished painters. One of whom was a woman of great talent...

Even if one ignores the best known writers and poets, a history of the Franco-American cultural exchange could easily fill a large volume. John Trumbull, who came to Paris in 1780, was the first in a long series of painters along with Samuel Morse, (better known as the inventor of the telegraph than as the painter of "La Fayette Afoot") John Vanderlyn, Rembrandt Peale or George Healy ; these three were among the best of America's portrait painters.

In 1788, the American Academy of Arts and Sciences was founded by Quesnay de Beaurepaire, Rochambeau's companion in arms. French classical architecture, much admired by Jefferson during his sojourn as ambassador to France, made its mark on American villages and towns. The engineer Pierre-Charles Lenfant, a soldier in the Revolutionary Army, designed Washington D.C., while William Strickland, the architect of the first Town Hall in New York, introduced to the United States the technique of the suspension bridge, which he had learned in France.

Woman reading Le Figaro, *by Mary Cassatt and* The Church of Saint-Nicolas-du-Chardonnet in Paris, *a sketch by Frank Boggs.*

In the second half of the XIXth century, study in Paris became a "must" for American artists. The Barbizon school of painting, made famous by Millet, had among its disciples William Morris Hunt and Edward Wheelwright. Corot influenced George Inness and Homer D. Martin ; Monet befriended Théodore Robinson who attracted many compatriots to Giverny. The most famous American students of the French masters were James Whistler, who studied in Gleyre's atelier before working with Fantin-Latour, Courbet, Degas and Manet; and Mary Cassatt, who in 1873, settled in Paris at age 29. Cassatt worked with Degas, Renoir and Pissaro, who envied her sketches. She was decorated with the Légion d'honneur in1904 ; she died in Paris in 1926. ∎

Commercial Exchanges

The treaty of 1778 was meant to develop "friendship and commerce" between France and the United States. In time, this double mission was accomplished, without it being clear whether sentimental or financial reasons played the greater role.

In Dr. Jacob's pharmacy on the corner of Peachtree and Marietta Streets in Atlanta, Georgia, "French coca wine," the future symbol of the "American way of life," made its debut in 1885. The beverage was renamed Coca Cola by its ingenious inventor John S. Pemberton, who wanted to distinguish his product from that of his competitor, the *Vin Mariani*. Pemberton's product was an ideal "pick-me-up." It soothed frayed nerves, cured headaches, asthenia, stomach cramps and other ailments. This miracle concoction, of which Pemberton only sold a few glasses a day, would someday conquer the world.

By June 1944, American troops had consumed more than five billion bottles of this "essence of America" since the beginning of World War II. Dozens of bottling factories were opened around the world, pumping out the beverage as fast as the G.I.s could drink it.

The liberated countries soon appreciated Coca Cola and chewing gum with as much enthusiasm as their new found liberty. ∎

LE TRAIT D'UNION

"Dear friend, have some Byrrh, to wash down all this water"

If French wines, perfumes, cheeses and certain mineral waters sell well in the United States, no product "Fabriqué en France" has come near the sales records of the "non-alcoholic beverage made from extracts of coca" by a genius named John S. Pemberton. It has never been for lack of trying, however, as this ad, published in the 30's, testifies.

La F

ette, we are here!

Bled all but white by three years of a murderous war, France appealed to America for help. The arrival of the "Sammies" would decide the outcome of the war.

Woodrow Wilson

The son of a Presbyterian minister, Thomas Woodrow Wilson was born in Staunton, Virginia, in 1856. Wilson was an attorney who later became professor of political science and president of Princeton University. In 1911, at the age of 55, Wilson was elected the Democratic governor of New Jersey. In the following year, he was elected president of the U.S.A. Wilson initiated a number of ambitious reforms : the election of senators by direct universal suffrage, a reduction in import taxes, the creation of an income tax, and the beginning of anti-trust legislation. When war erupted in Europe, Wilson, a confirmed pacifist, suggested mediation. Unfortunately, Colonel House, whom Wilson had appointed mediator, failed. On April 6, 1917, the United States entered the war. Wilson hoped that at the conflict's end, the United States would be in a position to negotiate a "New World Order" wherein nations could settle future disputes peacefully. But the weaknesses of the peace treaties and Congress's rejection of the League of Nations ended this dream. Woodrow Wilson died in 1924.

Thomas Woodrow Wilson was elected President of the United States on November 5, 1912. Wilson, a minister's son, was an ardent pacifist. He wanted to avoid, at all costs, the United States becoming embroiled in the erupting European conflict. As a child he had witnessed the horrors of the American Civil War ; and he feared a new conflict would mean a return that barbarity. Moreover, he worried about maintaining national unity in a country where one citizen in four had been born abroad, or whose parents had come from either of the opposing camps now forming in the Old World. Wilson had to act with extreme prudence : how could he take sides when Americans of German origin supported the Axis powers; when Anglo-Saxon Protestants on the East Coast supported the Allied powers ; when the Irish detested the English, and the Polish were hostile to the Russians?

Assigned the task of negotiating a peace between Paris, London and Berlin, American diplomat Colonel House went to Europe in the Spring of 1914. Then Archduke Francis Ferdinand was assassinated in Sarajevo; and all hope for this negotiated peace ended. The much feared conflict began on August 3, 1914. Over the next three years, in his role as a "neutral mediator," Wilson, launched several diplomatic initiatives to end the war. He suggested a plan for "Peace without victory," but none of the belligerents would consider it.

Then in May of 1915, a German U-boat torpedoed and sunk the British passenger ship "Lusitania." This altered the course of events. The United States strongly condemned the act ; there were 128 Americans among the Lusitania's 1,000 victims. These deaths moved public opinion in favor of the war. But a British publication naming American companies

FIRST IN FRANCE

U.S. MARINES

Previous two pages : An American offensive in the Somme in 1918. The enemy learned, in a series of painful lessons, that the Sammies' skills had been underestimated.

Mercredi 4 avril 1917. — N° 8956

LE JOURNAL

ÉDITION DE PARIS

CHARLES HUMBERT
Directeur

...UNIS PROCLAMENT L'ÉTAT DE GUERRE

AU CONGRÈS

Le Message du président Wilson

Le programme de M. Wilson acclamé par la majorité

Il demande à ses compatriotes de tendre toutes leurs forces pour écraser l'Allemagne

In the news-papers, as in the popular imagination, a similar joy : America, at last, comes to the aid of France!

le bienvenu

who had violated a trade boycott with the Germans, annoyed those who wished to remain out of the conflict. The coming elections of November 1916, which looked like a close race, meant that the President could not force the issue. But in January of 1917, the Germans decided, despite ongoing negotiations, to order their submarines to fire on American ships. This strengthened American resolve to fight the Axis. Wilson severed diplomatic relations with Berlin.

"The War to End All Wars"

He did not have long to wait for the next "act of intentional injustice." Soon after, the "Vigilentia" was torpedoed. On April 6, 1917, at 13:18, the United States Congress voted to go to war. The majority supported this decision, in part, because of the publication of the "Zimmerman telegram." The German Minister of War telegrammed his Mexican ambassador to prepare Mexico to join their alliance against the United States. The telegram suggested a similar alliance with Japan which further fueled American public

outrage. Though the Americans had chosen "the defense of law over that of peace," they were not well prepared for war. The American Army was very small, and its only troops with combat experience had fought the Indians, Filippino Insurgents, the Spanish in Cuba and Pancho Villa's Mexican outlaws . They hardly seemed capable of supporting the massive conflict on the far off battlefields of Europe. This explains the calm assurance with which the Kaiser declared, "If Wilson wants war, let him have it — and so much the worse for him." America, however, rose to the challenge.

In very little time, there was concrete evidence of its determination and efficacy. Despite what some Democrats called "another form of slavery," Congress approved the Selective Service Act on May 18, 1917. This Act conscripted all male citizens between the ages of 21 and 30 into the Armed Service. Thus the Army increased from 200,000 in February of 1917 to four million by November 1918.

In the meantime, a committee for public information organized meetings and demonstrations to convince

the public that the war was a just cause. The government sold War bonds which were promoted by famous film stars Douglas Fairbanks and Mary Pickford. The President decreed a "mobilization of every resource in the nation." Created at the end of 1917, the War Industries Bureau, under the direction of Bernard Baruch, took measures to control industrial production : the distribution of raw materials and sources of energy was organized in deference to the war effort ; industries were converted ; railways were placed under government control ; and the organization of food for Europe was administered by a mining engineer named Herbert Hoover.

The turning point

For the French, the American entry into the war came at the perfect moment : the fall of the Czar meant that the future role of Russia was uncertain ; and there was the bloody failure of the Nivelle offensive in the area of Chemin des Dames ; and finally the mutinies at the front gave even those most optimistic

reason to doubt. The news of the American intervention raised the soldiers' moral, and revived the government's hope that in time, "we will win."
In the Spring of 1917, when he took command of the French Army, which had been bled all but white by an extreme and reckless offensive strategy, General Pétain announced that he would wait for the "Americans and the tanks." The arrival en masse of the "Sammies," as the French called them, turned the tide in the Allies' favor. By the summer of 1918, two million American soldiers would be on French soil. As important as American military ground support, was the financial aid the United States contributed to the cause. The Allies had long before exhausted their funds, and only the United States Federal Treasury could afford to make such loans. When President Wilson announced, "America goes to war with all her force," it also meant that the Allied nations would obtain financial aid for the war effort ; this amounted to ten billion dollars between April, 1917 and June, 1920. Logistically, the American Navy was vital in the fight

Life and death on the Front.
Above : *The coffin of Private Osborn in Camp Châlons's chapel. Osborn was one of the first Americans killed in the Great War. The icons on the chapel's walls were left by Russian troops who had mutinied following the Bolshevik revolution in 1917.*

The La Fayette Squadron

Conceived in 1914 by three American pilots, the squadron of U.S. volunteers came into being on April 18, 1916, in the East of France. Registered as the N 124 and commanded by captain Thénault, it was issued six Nieuport 11s. The pilots were American. Many had had to join the Foreign Legion to qualify. On April 23, Kiffin Rockwell knocked out a German LVG. Stationed at Bar-le-Duc, the squadron shot down 13 enemy planes, and lost just one of their own. On May 24, Lufbery joined N 124. His 17 victories made him an ace. In Nieuport 17s, the Americans fought in the battle of the Somme. Later they were issued Spad VIIs. The squadron was baptized "La Fayette" on December 6, 1916, and took on von Richthofen's "Circus" in Flanders before being deployed to Verdun. In 1918, the La Fayette Squadron became part of the American forces as the103rd Aero Squadron. At the armistice, the 30 pilots who had flown under its banner had totalled 199 hits, of which 57 were confirmed fatal. Employed again in 1939-40, it destroyed 74 enemy aircraft.

against the German U-Boat blockade. The construction of new ships, the work of the American Merchant Marine and the capture of German ships anchored in the previously neutral ports of Latin America, made marine transport, which had been seriously limited, available to the Allied Forces.

During his visit to the United States in April of 1917, Marshal Joffre explained how desperate the situation remained : three years of bloody combat had weakened the Anglo-French alliance, fresh troops were desperately needed. The French could quickly equip and train these troops in the combat skills required for trench warfare. France thus provided the American Expeditionary Force with : 75 and 155 mm canons ; 155 mm shells, all of its tanks ; 81% of the airplanes ; more than half of its long range canons ; 57,000 machine guns ; ten million shells ; and more than 200 million bullets.

The Doughboys go "Over There"

One hundred seventy seven Americans of the Expeditionary Force, including the commanding officer General Pershing and Lieutenant Patton, arrived at Boulogne-sur-Mer on June 13, 1917. They were welcomed by the Allies' highest ranking military representatives and Colonel Jacques Aldebert de Chambrun (who, like all direct descendants of the Marquis de La Fayette, automatically possessed American citizenship). Pershing, Patton and their men went directly to Paris where they met with the Minister of War Paul Painlevé, Marshal Joffre, and General Foch. In Paris, the Americans received an unprecedented reception : the people

A French Spad VII from the Stork Squadron

mobbed the streets of the capital to cheer the soldiers as they marched to the Place de la Concorde. General Pershing had to appear at the balcony of the *Hôtel Crillon* before the crowd agreed to disperse.

Two weeks later on June 28,1917, 14,000 American soldiers arrived at the port of Saint-Nazaire : there were 13,000 men in the 1st division (the famous "Big Red One") and a battalion of the 5th Marine regiment — soldiers who their commander had planned to send immediately to camps for several months of training. The French, however insisted that the "Sammies" celebrate the 141st anniversary of the signing of the Declaration of Independence. The 16th Infantry regiment was chosen to march in the parade ; the soldiers were covered by flowers thrown by hundreds of thousands of Parisians.

"La Fayette, nous voilà !"

On his ceremonial visit to the tomb of La Fayette, Pershing, a better soldier than an orator, asked Captain Stanton to say a few words on his behalf. There were just four : "La Fayette, nous voilà !."

Immediately, the crowd at Picpus cemetery unleashed a riotous and joyful cheer which, to this day, echoes throughout the world.

Pershing refused an amalgamation of the inexperienced American troops and the battle-toughened French or British soldiers. President Wilson and Pershing agreed that the American Army should retain its own identity ; once prepared and strong enough, the Americans would play their own role in the common effort.

At the end of July, the 1st division began training near Langres, in the Haute-Marne region, east of Paris. In September, they were joined by the 26th division, composed mostly of National Guard members from New England. Then a brigade of Marines arrived ; they were soon followed by the 2nd division. This division included : an infantry brigade of regulars ; three artillery regiments ; a civil engineering regiment ; and a battalion of radio transmission soldiers. In October, the 42nd division arrived. It was known

John Pershing

When John Joseph Pershing landed at Boulogne in France, on June 13, 1917, he already had a prestigious career behind him. Born in 1860, he had attended Nebraska University. He later taught at West Point. He fought the Apaches with the 6th Cavalry before commanding Sioux scouts in the Dakotas. He further distinguished himself during the campaign against Cuba in 1898 ; in 1903, he was ordered to the Philippines to put down the Moros rebellion. Appointed military attaché to Japan in 1905, he was promoted to Brigadier-General the following year. He then returned to the Philippines as Governor. In 1916, he directed the campaign against Pancho Villa, but just as he was to assume command of the troops, he received orders to go to the battlefields of Europe. Despite his lack of experience in large-scale conflicts, he was more than equal to the task.

In October, the 42nd division arrived. It was known as the "Rainbow Division" because its soldiers, all from the National Guard, came from twenty six different states.

"Sammies" in "Looneyville"

Pershing had very little time to prepare the American Expeditionary Force for battle. By the end of October 1917, the 1st division was given a region near Toul and Lunéville, soon called "Looneyville" by the American troops.

At the request of Marshal Foch, who had recently been promoted to commander-in-chief of the Allied forces, the other three divisions were deployed to contain the German's Spring offensive which threatened to break through the Front.

The 28th regiment of the 1st Division fought south of Amiens near the village of Cantigny, where they took the territory without much difficulty. Despite

Mr. Newton Baker, the American Secretary of War, inspecting the front with General Pershing and his staff, in 1918.

seven fierce German counter attacks, which included violent bombardments and canisters of the infamous "mustard gas," the "Sammies" held their ground. In just one battle, they had proven to the Germans that they should not be underestimated.

In June and July, the superb action at Bois-Belleau of the American 2nd division and Marines, re-enforced by French colonial troops, demonstrated their capacity to counter a major German offensive. Through

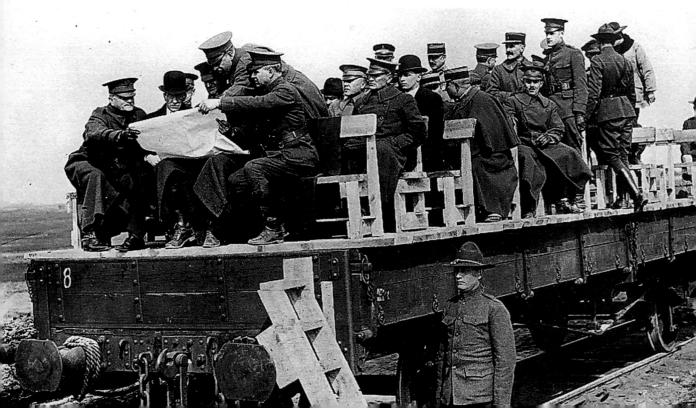

their combined efforts these troops managed, for three long weeks, to block all enemy movements towards Paris.

When the French decided to launch a counter-offensive on July 18, from the Champagne region, 85,000 Americans stood by for combat. Pershing wanted his troops to have a large victory of their own under the Stars and Stripes. This victory came during the major offensive of September, 1918.

On September 12, at 05:00 after a long artillery bombardment using 3,000 canons, seven American divisions under Generals Dickmann, Ligget and Cameron, charged the Saint-Mihiel bulge assisted by the French 2nd colonial corps.

"A Magnificent Victory"

At the end of the combat, 16,000 Germans were taken prisoner, and more than 300 canons were confiscated. Foch congratulated Pershing, "The American Ist Army, under your command, has managed a magnificent victory with a plan of action that was as carefully conceived as it was magnificently executed."

The next offensive, launched at the end of the month, in the Argonne region, became a mud bath because of the incessant rain.

Pershing wrote of this operation : "Under the icy rain in these dark nights, our civil engineers not only have to build new roads over terrain made sponge-like by shelling, but they must also repair the damaged roads and build bridges over flooded rivers. Our artillery, thinking not of sleep, moves hand-pulled carts through deep mud and clay, to bring the equipment necessary to support the infantry."

Badly nourished, subjected to constant enemy bombardments, confronted with appalling weather conditions and stuck on difficult terrain, Ligget's troops held their position while threatened from all sides.

Fortunately the Germans weakened and the 197 divisions they had on paper, could not resist the 220 Allied divisions.

Moreover, the 42 American divisions were now recei-

George Patton

When General John Pershing took command of the American Expeditionary Forces in Europe, he knew he could count on Captain George Smith Patton. Born in 1885, the young Californian had graduated from West Point in 1909. Patton was an athlete ; he made the pentathlon team for the 1912 Stockholm Olympics. An experienced soldier, he had fought under Pershing in the campaign against Pancho Villa in 1916 (This was the United States Army's first motorized combat). But his love for and knowledge of France were Patton's most important qualities : he had taken fencing classes at the prestigious Saumur Cavalry School, both he and his wife spoke French fluently. Patton arrived with Pershing on June 13, 1917. By September 1, 1917, he had established headquarters in Chaumont, in the Haute-Marne. He studied French tanks at Champlieu and returned to Langres to begin training Americans to use them. On September 12, 1918, his 304th tank brigade took part in the liberation of Saint-Mihiel. Promoted to Lt-Colonel, Patton was injured on September 26th. On October 17th, he was promoted again to full Colonel. He was decorated for Distinguished Service just before the armistice. Twenty six years later, he played a major role in the liberation of Western Europe.

ving 250,000 re-enforcements each month. These re-enforcements added to the two million "Sammies" already deployed by the end of 1918.

When the armistice was finally signed on November 11, 1918 in the Compiègne forest, it brought to an end the bloodiest conflict in human history — collectively the war cost nearly 8,500,000 lives and 30 million more had been injured — 50,000 Americans had died on French soil.

A Rendez-vous with Death

Among those casualties was the poet Alan Seeger, who had been a volunteer in the French Foreign Legion since the beginning of the conflict.

Several days before he met Death, the centerpiece of his poetry, he wrote, "We are leaving for another assault tomorrow. This will probably be the toughest I have ever seen. We have been given the honor to be on the front line. No duffel bag, but a backpack, a canvas sheet hanging off one shoulder, lots of cartridges and hand grenades, as well as a bayonet on the end of our rifle. I am happy to be in the first assault wave. If you must go into battle, it is best to be thrown in completely. That is the supreme experience."

On July 4, 1916, Alan Seeger kept his rendez-vous : he was killed in action and became the symbol of the young Americans who sacrificed their lives in the name of Liberty. ∎

Opposite : *July 4, 1917, on the rue de Rivoli. The "Sammies" proudly march before the ecstatic Parisians in celebration of American Independence day. After this parade, General Pershing visited La Fayette's tomb in the Picpus cemetery. The enthusiastic welcome given to the troops of the American Expeditionary Force, attested to the hope their arrival brought to the Allied soldiers.*

Douglas MacArthur

Everyone recalls General MacArthur's, "I shall return," when in 1942, he left the Philippines to escape the Japanese offensive. Less well known is that this old soldier began his military career in France during World War I. The future hero of Corregidor was in the vanguard when the 84th infantry brigade led the charge on Saint-Mihiel in September of 1918. For his his leadership and bravery — he was exposed to mustard gas and shot at — he soon became commander of the 42nd Division. After the Armistice, he became head of West Point Military Academy ; he had graduated from the Academy, first in his class, just fifteen years earlier. Promoted in January of 1925, the 45 year-old native of Little Rock, Arkansas, became the youngest General in the American Army. In 1930, President Herbert Hoover appointed him Army Chief of Staff. Then, in July 1941, President Franklin D. Roosevelt made him commanding general of U.S. forces in the Far East. But that is another story...

Doctor Jazz

In 1918, after four excruciatingly painful years of war,
France discovered a royal remedy for the "blues" :
Black American music.

Chief Sergeant Noble Sissle, better known as a violinist than the drum Major of the 369th United States infantry unit, wrote this inspired description of the arrival of Jazz in France : "Lt. Europe, before raising his baton, twitched his shoulders, apparently to be sure his tight-fitting military uniform would stand the strain, each musician shifted his feet, the players of brass horns blew the saliva from their instruments, the drummers tightened their drumheads, everyone settled back in their seats, and when the baton came down with a swoop, both the director and musicians seemed to forget their surroundings ; they were lost in scenes and memories. Cornet and clarinet players began to manipulate notes in that typical rhythm (which no artist has ever been able to put down on paper) ; as the drummers struck their stride, their shoulders began shaking in time to their syncopated raps. Then, it seemed, the whole audience began to sway, dignified French officers began to tap their feet along with the American general, who, temporarily, had lost his style and grace. Lt. Europe was no longer the Lt. Europe of a moment ago, but once more Jim

Noble Sissle and Jimmy Europe had played together in civilian life (top, right), before bringing Jazz to France as soldiers (above and below).

Europe who, a few months ago, rocked New York with his syncopated baton. He turned to the trombone players, who sat impatiently waiting for their cue to have

a "jazz spasm" and they drew their slides out and jerked them back with that characteristic "crack". The audience could stand it no longer ; the "jazz germ" hit them. "There now, I said to myself, Colonel Hayward has brought his band over here and started "rag-timeitis" in France ; ain't this an awful thing to visit upon a nation with so many burdens ! But when the band had finished and the people were roaring with laughter, I was forced to say that this is just what France needs at this moment. But the thing that capped the climax happened up in Northern France : we were playing in a little village. Among the crowd, listening to that band, was an old lady about 60 years of age. To everyone's surprise, all of a sudden, she started doing a dance that resembled "Walking the Dog". Then I was cured, and statisfied that American music would some day be the world's music." ∎

France and America, Partners for Peace

In 1928, ten years after World War I, France and America united to ban armed conflict forever. Even though it was hailed as the dawn of a new age of universal peace, the "Kellogg-Briand Pact" could not defuse the antagonisms that would become World War II.

"**N**ever again!" In 1927, France and Germany were on a honeymoon unimaginable a year before. As President Wilson had hoped, the League of Nations worked vigorously for the foundation of universal peace. Despite their ascent to the rank of a world power, the United States had returned to its pre-war isolationism. The country that had inspired the League of Nations was not even a member!

In April, on the tenth anniversary of America's entry into World War I, Aristide Briand made a remarkable speech inviting the United States to become more involved in European affairs. Briand, a much respected politician, had been President of the French Council several times before being appointed Minister of Foreign Affairs by successive governments on both the Left and the Right. Briand's speech came at an opportune moment. Preparations for the conference to discuss disarmament were going badly. And the problem of French war debts weighed on the Franco-American relationship. In June of 1927, Briand proposed to American Secretary of State Frank Kellogg that their nations sign a pact of mutual renunciation of war. Secretary Kellogg readily accepted. This accord, purely symbolic, would unite their two nations in peace and friendship; in time it would grow to include every nation on earth. The "Kellogg-Briand Pact," as it was called, was signed on February 6, 1928 by France and the United States. It prohibited recourse to war as a political instrument. There were no sanctions planned other than the censure of the other signatories. But as one newspaper editor noted, "at least the moral conscience will act as a serious obstacle to those wishing to break the agreement."

A. Briand signing the pact that, as one newspaper put it, "consumates his honeymoon with peace."

The accord remained in Washington DC, under the protection of the United States, where it would stay until future adherents signed. The Kellogg-Briand Pact was eventually ratified by 63 countries, including Germany, the British Empire, Japan, Poland, Italy and Czechoslovakia. For their work toward world peace, both the French and the American statesmen were awarded the Nobel prize. ∎

The Golden Age of the "French Line"

More peaceful, but just as enthusiastically fought as the sea battles of the previous war,
the "Blue Ribbon" race mobilized ship-builders, engineers, and sailors
of the period between the two wars.

Although France had produced Denis Papin and Marc Isambard Brunel, creator of the gigantic steamship, *The Great Eastern*

and Frédéric Sauvage, who invented the spinning propeller, Samuel Cunard's British steamers ruled the seas in the XIXth century.

In 1935, France finally surpassed, once and for all, her ancient maritime rival by launching the sumptuous *Normandie* oceanliner — a veritable sailing city.

The *Normandie* was the biggest, the most beautiful, and the fastest civilian ship to ever sail between Paris and New York : 313 meters long, 36 meters wide at the level of the promenade deck, 39 meters high from the base of the keel to the roof of the bridge, she weighed 83,000 tons and could move at speeds of up to thirty knots (nearly 40 miles per hour).

She was equipped with a 160,000 horsepower engine. Fitted with the latest innovations, the flagship of the Compagnie Générale Transatlantique possessed all the refined luxuries one would expect of a French ship. A journalist wrote, "the dining room is 86 meters long and nine and a half meters high — the same dimensions as the hall of mirrors in Versailles — enclosed by plates of cut glass, with a fantastic gilt ceiling, a dream setting where, by the soft light of the wall lamps, 150 tables are arranged to serve as many as 700 people sumptuous feasts..." There was also a café that opened onto the sea, a dance floor, a main passenger lounge in which hung superb Aubusson tapestries, fashion boutiques, a florists' shop, a gymnasium, a massage and hydrotherapy center, a book shop, a thea-

ter which accommodated 400 where the latest "talkies" were projected, a swimming pool lined with white enamel, and a chapel where the stations of the Cross were carved in wood... Catering to the passengers of the ship's 2,000 cabins were 187 cooks, nine butchers, ten bakers and 688 waiters.

At mid-day, on June 3, 1935, a huge crowd gathered at New York harbor's pier 88 to welcome the *Normandie*. After a voyage of four days, two hours and twelve minutes, at an average speed of almost 30 knots, she set a new record that won her the "Blue Ribbon," the coveted trophy that went to the fastest vessel to cross the North Atlantic. And at this same port, on February 9, 1942, after 150 flawless crossings, a fire ended the career of this seafaring giant. Renamed *La Fayette*, and transformed into a troop transport ship, were it not for this accident, she would have served more modestly, but more importantly the cause of Franco-American friendship. ∎

The Normandie, *flagship of the French Line and winner of the coveted "Blue Ribbon," left the British Cunard oceanliners in its wake.*

Musical Exchanges

A young Black American dancer conquers Paris with the wild new rhythms of the charleston; a handsome young Parisian crooner takes Hollywood by storm. They became overnight sensations in each other's land.

Despite his Hollywood success, Maurice Chevalier preferred Paris. He did, however, continue his international career.

Born in Saint Louis, Missouri, in 1906, Josephine Baker began her career as a chorus girl. She was noticed by an agent who wanted to bring her to Paris: "But Mrs. Dudley, what would I do? Dance the charleston? Oh! There's nothing simpler! You just toss your legs and arms in all directions with all your heart !" Josephine arrived on an October morning in 1925, at Saint-Lazare station. André Davan, the director of the *Théâtre des Champs-Elysées*, recalled that as he waited for the dancers of the *Revue Nègre*, he saw : "From under an extravagant hat, in black and white check overalls, a long and supple young lady who stood out from the motley crowd, approached us and said, "and so this is Paris!" These were her first words before the conquest. Conquest *is* the word ! Soon "La Baker" was on the front pages of all the papers. Some praised this miracle from Harlem. Others deplored the scandalously primitive show. Paul Colin, the artist who designed the show's poster, made Josephine its centerpiece. Years later he still remembered how she danced, "naked, belted up in an outfit of green feathers... frenetic, undulating and moved by the ecstatic sound of the saxophones." France adopted Josephine and she, in turn accepted her new country and settled in Paris. World War II interrupted her outstanding career. She enlisted in the Free French Army. At War's end, Lieutenant Baker was decorated by de Gaulle. An indefatigable fighter for universal brotherhood, she adopted children of all races and nationalities. To support them she resumed her triumphant career at the age of 60. She died in April of 1975.

Hollywood's Parisian

"I kissed my friends good-bye. As I sailed from Le Havre, I thought about Georges Carpentier who had gone to America to fight Dempsey. I prefer my thing to his : the falls aren't quite so brutal !" His "thing" was singing, and a little acting after MGM had given him a screen test. His name — Maurice Chevalier — was soon on every cinema marquee in America. Chevalier starred in Ernst Lubitsch's *Love Parade*. The film was a triumph, and the beginning of a fabulous career for this consummate Parisian whose style and accent seduced American audiences. In 1935, he returned to France to resume his career as a singer with even greater success. ■

Lindbergh Conquers the Atlantic

May 21, 1927, 22:19. The United States and France make history when Charles Lindbergh lands The Spirit of Saint Louis *at the Bourget airfield near Paris after a flight of thirty three hours and twenty seven minutes.*

"I'm turning and slightly reducing the fuel ; I'm slowly beginning the descent... I'm now circling. Yes, I see an airport below. I can make out a section of a concrete runway in front of a half-opened hangar door... I'm 400 meters above the runway. I'm now reducing the fuel and turning to make my final approach."

Charles Lindbergh, who after this achievement, would be affectionately known to Americans as "Lucky Lindy," smoothly landed on French soil. He had just completed the first non-stop flight from New York to Paris.

The flight covered a distance of 3,600 miles in 33 hours and 27 minutes : an average of 116 miles per hour. Lucky Lindy might not have been the first to make the flight. Just twelve days earlier, Charles Nungesser and François Coli, two French pilots, disappeared with their plane, *L'Oiseau Blanc*, as they attempted the flight in the opposite direction. But the crowds that rushed to Bourget from Paris, enthusiastically greeted the young American, who had just conquered the Atlantic. "The French met me with an indescribable warmth and excitement... While I was circling the airport, I had no idea that the traffic jam below were the people rushing to greet me. I couldn't believe it when thousands of people jumped the airport fence and rushed towards the plane as soon as I landed. I had just cut the motor when the first group got to the plane. Then in what seemed like a second, I was surrounded by folks shouting my name in a foreign accent..."

The 25 year-old pilot from Detroit, Michigan was welcomed by Mr. Myron T. Herrick, the American Ambassador to France. Young Lindy had won the hearts and fired the imaginations of the Parisians.

When he was received at the *Hôtel de Ville*, Paris' City Hall, nearly half a million people gathered to cheer as he rode by. Marshals Foch and Joffre praised his courage, and President Gaston Domergue awarded him France's highest honor : the *Légion d'Honneur*. General Gouraud declared, "Not only have you united two continents, but also the hearts of people everywhere, in admiration for the simple courage of a man who accomplished a great thing."

On May 8, 1927, Frenchmen Charles Nungesser and François Coli attempted an Atlantic crossing in their amphibious plane, L'Oiseau Blanc. They were never heard from again. Nungesser, a flying ace in World War I, and credited with bringing down 45 enemy planes, was an experienced pilot. Coli was also an experienced aviator. In 1919, he had made the first round trip across the Mediterranean.

When Charles Lindbergh arrived in Paris, he was heartily congratulated by Louis Blériot. Eighteen years before, the French aviator had been the first to pilot a plane across the English Channel.

June 6, 1944, 21:00. The liberation of Europe has begun.
And as in 1918, the United States will play a decisive role.

he Name of Liberty

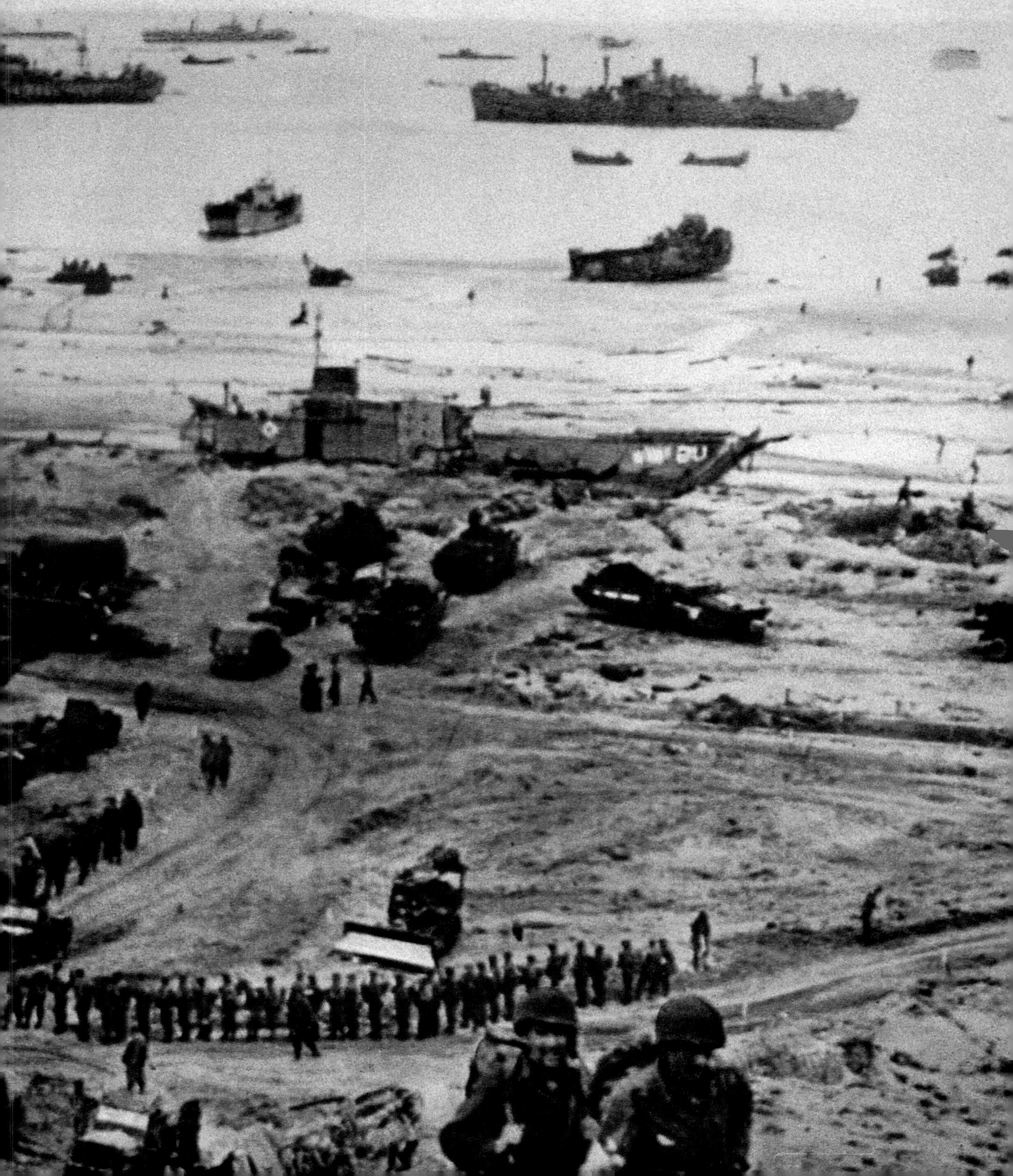

Very carefully planned for months and preceded by a monumental aerial bombardment, Operation Overlord was considered a success by dusk on D-Day. East of the landing zone, the English and Canadians had established beachheads. To the West, despite the 1st and 29th infantry divisions' dreadful losses during the landing at Omaha Beach, the American Ist Army division had solid possession of the beach. At Utah Beach, the 4th infantry division managed to land without much difficulty, although they did have problems in the marshes beyond the beach. As for the 82nd and 101st Airborne, the landing in Sainte-Mère-Église was confused. Ironically, the vast dispersal of the US paratroopers helped to surprise the enemy; they didn't know where to concentrate their defensive efforts. While General Dempsey's English and Canadian troops progressed very slowly against the Germans' Panzer units, the Americans successfully reached their objectives in good time in the weeks that followed. The capture of Isigny and Carentan opened the road to Cotentin. Despite the actions of the 17th SS Panzer division, "Götz von Berlichingen," the Allied troops had by June 18th, reached the West coast of the peninsula. By the end of the month, the American Ist Army had taken Cherbourg. Unfortunately the port installations had been mined by the Germans before their surrender. And the fierce storm that had hit the prefabricated concrete ports built offshore Arromanche and

Despite serious losses, the Allies did get a foothold on the beaches. That paratroopers were dropped behind the Front, so confused the enemy, it threw their defense plans into disarray; nor were they able to get re-enforcements.

Dwight Eisenhower

Dwight David Eisenhower was born, into a family of German origin, in Denison, Texas in 1890. He graduated from West Point in 1915 where he had specialized in armored warfare. He received his orders to report to France, just as the Armistice was signed. When his career was not taking the direction he had planned, Eisenhower considered leaving the Army. In 1935 MacArthur summoned Eisenhower to the Philippines. He excelled at organization and logistics — qualities that prompted his superiors to send him to headquarters rather than to the battlefields, despite his preference for the opposite. He was promoted to the rank of Major in March of 1942. General Marshall then assigned him to come up with an Allied strategy in Europe. He was charged with the planning of the invasion of Normandy which, if successful, would lead to the liberation of Europe. Having outlined his plan and strategies to General Marshall, Eisenhower was surprised to hear, "Are you happy with the work you have done? Good! because the Supreme Commander of the Allied forces in Europe is you!"

...of D-Day landing's biggest coups was the seizure of the Pointe du ...it was a steep cliff 30 meters high, on which sat a German strong-...midst a network of tunnels. Colonel Rudder's American Rangers ...this precipice. In this mission, 135 American soldiers were killed.

Bloody Omaha

The sector of Omaha Beach on which the Americans had to land was six kilometers wide, and extremely well defended by the Germans. General Bradley recalls the first moments of this intense combat :

"The first men jumped into the water under the enemy crossfire. Many were injured by the first shots. Others drowned. Those who made it to the beach were under such strong machine gun fire that they couldn't stay on the beach, and had to move back to the water...Ten minutes after the ramps of the landing crafts dropped, an entire company was out of action for the rest of the battle. All the officers were killed or injured."

In those terrible hours, 'Bloody Omaha' earned her sinister name."

Omaha Beaches, had revealed their weaknesses. But the skill and determination of the American Army Corps of Engineers put Cherbourg Port back in service in even less time than the most optimist estimates. One port could not arm and supply the entire Allied war machine, which, by August numbered nearly two million men, 500,000 vehicles and three million tons of equipment. It was therefore urgent to move toward Brittany and take the coast ; in this way, the Allies would control a large enough section of the English Channel and the Atlantic, to facilitate access to the sea. For several weeks, the Americans fought the "battle of the hedgerows," over terrain that favored defensive positions and did not permit the use of superior, but massive weaponry. By the end of June, the Americans had lost 22,000 men. On July 18th, several days after the English had taken Caen, Saint-Lô, which the Germans had defended fiercely, fell to the Americans. From then on, General Omar Bradley, Commander of the American Ist Army, could penetrate enemy lines and shove the Germans South. Operation Cobra, launched the following week, realized this plan.

Operation Cobra

General Patton, commander of the IIIrd American Army, deployed the 4th and 6th armored divisions towards Coutances. Coutances was captured on July 28th, and Granville on July 30th. The following day, Avranches was also under American control. Moving now in longer strides, the American tanks seized Pontaubault and its bridge over the Sélune; this opened the road to the Loire and Brittany. Inspired by Patton's continuous drive, the 8th corps had made the legendary "Avranches breakthrough" which was fully exploited to give a new pace to the Battle of Normandy. The Americans, returning German fire in kind, captured in succession: Rennes, Vannes and Saint-Malo. Brest did not fall until September18th ; and even though the Germans did hold on to several "Atlantic enclaves" until the Spring of 1945, the remainder of Brittany was liberated. Rather than move southeast

Omar Bradley

Omar Bradley was born in Missouri in1893. He was a railroad worker before receiving a scholarship to attend the West Point Military Academy. After having graduated from West Point in 1915, Bradley taught at Fort Benning's infantry school. At Fort Benning, General Marshall appreciated the young man's organizational skills and in1943, sent him to join General Eisenhower in North Africa. Initially second in command on the Tunisian front, Bradley was soon made commander of the Second Army Corps when Patton was charged with the invasion of Sicily. After an illustrious campaign in Tunisia and Sicily, Bradley took command of the First Army Corps. After the successful invasion of Normandy, he took command of the Ist Army, now under the command of Hodges and of Patton's IIIrd Army. General Patton would now take orders from the man who had recently been his subordinate! Bradley initiated operation "Cobra," which permitted Patton to capture Avranches. On August 1st, General Bradley assumed command of the12th American Army Corps and now took his orders directly from Eisenhower. Bradley successfully pushed back the German counter attack at Mortain. But he was criticized for having forced Patton to stop at Argentan instead joining the Canadians at Crerrar. Had Patton's troops been able to join the Canadians, they could have completely surrounded a German stronghold, already partially trapped in the Mortain enclave. Supported by General Simpson's IXth Army, Bradley's troops liberated a major portion of France, and continued straight up to the Ardennes to meet the German counter offensive, the famous Battle of the Bulge. They crossed the Rhine and surrounded the Ruhr, finally ended their unbroken progression at the Elbe river. General Omar Bradley was head of the Joint Chiefs of Staff during the Korean War. He died in New York in 1981.

along the coast, the Allies decided to push the offensive northwest and liberate the Channel ports in the Pas-de-Calais. By September, General Montgomery's British troops had advanced as far as Anvers. In the meantime, General Patton wanted to surround the German forces to the south of Normandy and encircle them in the Falaise enclave. The Germans were not completely beaten, but they were cornered. During this battle, General Leclerc's legendary 2nd French armored division which had been integrated into Patton's IIIrd Army, took a decisive role in the liberation of Alençon. Patton's 79th infantry division

An American's Account of the Liberation

Gertrude Stein, the mother of American literary modernism, had settled in Paris in 1903. During W.W.I, as a volunteer with the American Fund for the French Wounded, she drove food and medical supplies between bases in the south of France. In 1940, despite pressure from both French and American friends, she refused to abandon her adopted country. Stein spent 4 anxious years in two small villages near the Alps. Here, in an excerpt from *Wars I Have Seen*, she recalls her joy at the news that the Americans had finally come :

"The Americans are at Aix-les-Bains, only 25 kilometers away how we want to see them even a little more than the rest of the population which is saying a great deal. We found some American flag ribbon in the local country store, and we gave it to all the little boys, just as we did in the 1914-1918 war [...] Vive la France vive l'Amérique vive les alliés vive Paris, after this most exciting day[...] An F.F.I. [a member of the French Resistance] said to me there is a train of your compatriots standing at a siding just below [...] I went quickly [...] I said Hello to the first group and they said Hello and I said I am an American and they laughed and said so were they and how did I hapen to be caught here [...] and I told them who I was thinking some of them might have heard of me but lots of them had and they crowded around and we talked and talked [...] Yes they were American boys but they had a poise and competely lacked the provincialism which did characterize the last American army, they talked and they listened and they had a sureness, they were quite certain of themselves [...] They are intereted, they are observant, they are accustomed to various types of people and ways of being, they have plenty of curiosity, but not any criticism [...] There is one thing in which this army is not different from that other army that is in being generous and sweet and particularly kind to the children [...] One day one of the mothers in the town told me that her nine year old daughter had been praying every single day that she might see an American soldier and she never had and now her mother was beginning to be afraid that the child would lose her faith in prayer. I said I would take her down to see the American soldiers and we went. Naturally, they were sweet and each one of them thought of something to give her [...] And she was so happy, she sang them all the old French songs, *Clair de la Lune*, *The Good King Dagobert* and *On the Bridge of Avignon*. Then as we were going home I said to her, about that chewing gum you must chew it but be careful not to swallow it. Oh yes I know she said. How do you know that I asked oh she said because when there was the last war my mother was a little girl and the American soldiers gave her chewing gum and all through this war my mother used to tell us about it, and she gave a rapturous sigh and said now I have it."

moved first to Dreux, then to Mantes-la-Jolie and finally reached the Seine by August 19th. Initially, the Americans had planned to skirt around Paris to the north and south and not take it by force; but the vicious civil war that raged in the capital's streets convinced Eisenhower and Bradley to let Leclerc take the city. At 21:00 on August 24, 1944, every bell in Paris rang to celebrate General Leclerc's arrival at the *Hôtel de Ville* with the first detachment of the second armored division. On August 25th von Choltitz surrendered. Charles De Gaulle made his now famous speech: "Paris ! Paris outragé ! Paris brisé ! Libéré par lui-même, libéré par son peuple avec le concours des armées de la France!" (Paris ! Paris raped ! Paris broken ! Liberated by herself, liberated by her people with the help of the armies of France!"

Among the first of Paris' liberators was the writer Ernest Hemingway. He had done his best writing in the Paris of the 1920's. But in 1944, he immediately visited his old friend Pablo Picasso and offered him a gift… a case of hand grenades! (Hemingway also took credit for liberating the bar at the Ritz Hotel). Meanwhile, the 20th US Army corps seized Melun and Fontaine-bleau, and the 12th army corps, under General Patton, liberated Orléans on August 17th, Chartres on the 18th, Sens on the 21st and Troyes on the 26th.

While events in the North moved quickly, with Bradley's Ist and IIIrd Armies heading north and east, on August 15, General Patch landed in the south, near Cavalaire, on the coast of Maures and Estérel . Toulon and Marseilles were taken one month earlier than expected, due to the courage of the newly re-organized French Army. By September 3rd, Lyons had been liberated and on the 12th, the Allied forces from Operation Overlord and Operation "Anvil Dragoon " (The code name for the landing in Provence) met in Montbard, near Dijon in Burgundy. The pace of the Allied offensive quickly accelerated. Nancy fell, then Epinal. Up near Metz, the Allied troops had to stop — the victim of its own success. Allied headquarters had not calculated such a quick advance, and logistical

Antoine de Saint-Exupéry

July 31, 1944, 08: 45. The Lightning F-5B #223 takes off from Bastia Borgo, Corsica on a reconnaissance mission east of Lyon. At 14:30 the airplane, which by then would have run out of fuel, had not returned to base. Antoine de Saint-Exupéry had, somewhere between the sky and the sea, met the death of "fire and ice," that the hero of his *Fighter Pilot* so keenly desired. "Saint-Ex" may have been shot down in mid-day near Saint-Raphael by Lieutenant Heichele's Focke-Wulf 190 D-9. Saint-Exupéry was a pilot unlike any other. A gifted writer, who also pioneered air mail, Saint-Exupéry recorded this history in *Night Flight* and *Southern Mail*. When the War broke out, he joined the most dangerous reconnaissance unit, 2/33. Flying behind enemy lines, this unit lost 17 of its 23 planes. Saint-Exupéry's best known work is the enchanting story, *The Little Prince*.  Published during the War, the poetic beauty of its prose made *The Little Prince* an immediate classic. In 1941, Saint-Exupéry went to New York to persuade the United States to come to France's aid. When his "American friends" finally took up their arms to fight for France's liberty, Saint-Exupéry fought at their side, just as his ancestor Georges Alexandre Césarée de Saint-Exupéry (author of *War Notebooks*) had when he joined his compatriot La Fayette, in America's fight for independence.

problems grew increasingly worse. From September 29th to October 4th, Patton had to resist a German counter offensive in Nancy. The enemy was forced back and Patton moved on to the Saar river and the Siegfried line. Metz was finally captured on November 15 th ; Leclerc, now part of the American VIIth Army, moved on to Strasbourg. While the Americans marched toward the Rhine, and then to the Ruhr, which they took with the British,

the Germans had begun a massive counter offensive through the Ardennes. Operation "Autumn Fog," conceived by Adolf Hitler himself, began on December 16. Middleton's American 8th corps suffered the brunt of the Panzers that were sent to the Meuse. In several hours, the American Front was dislodged and had had to retreat nearly 30 kilometers. Three days later, Patton and Eisenhower organized a flank counter attack. The operation was risky but a fearless General Patton successfully moved the IIIrd Army to the northwest and launched a rescue mission to Mac Auliffe's 101st Airborne which was defending Bastogne. On December 26th, the surrounded paratroopers finally received help from the American 4th armored division. The weather improved, which enabled the Americans to exploit their control of the skies and to attack the enemy from the air. Soon after, the lack of fuel for their tanks put an end to the Germans' final offensive. The Allies' eastward advance could now continue. To the south, the 6th group of American armies and the First French Army of de Lattre de Tassigny destroyed the Colmar enclave. The men of the 9th armored division of the Ist army reached the Rhine, north of Coblenz, on March 7, 1945. General Hodges led the 9th and seized the bridge at Remagen. At 16:00 on April 25, at Torgau-on-Elbe, the men of the Ist American Army met the Soviet Army. On the 7th of May, 1945, at 02:45, the Third Reich surrendered at Reims. This time the sacrifices were greater, but as they had in 1918, the United States played a decisive role in the final victory. Once again, Europe was greatly indebted to the United States. ■

For the French Resistance, D-Day signaled the start of open rebellion against the occupying army. Throughout the country, French men and women, old and young, carried arms to help the Allied soldiers. They harassed the Germans, sabotaged trains and disrupted systems of communication whenever and wherever possible to thwart the enemy.

Doctor Jazz (Part Two)

In the Twenties, France chased the blues of the Great War to the rhythms of ragtime and the charleston. The "Zazous" of 1946 tried to forget the Occupation with be-bop. By 1946, "jass" had become jazz, and it was still the best remedy for the blues.

Saint-Germain-des-Prés, that "little kingdom whose borders are marked by three cafés and a church," — whose Prince, Boris Vian — when he wasn't Vernon Sullivan, the pseudonym he assumed when he published scandalous books that he claimed he had translated from the American — became after the War what Montparnasse had been in the "crazy years" between the wars. It was a mecca for artists from around the world, especially Ameri-cans, and above all if they were musicians. The list of "guest stars" at the jazz clubs the Tabou the Saint-Germain, where young Parisians, so long deprived of simple freedoms and pleasure, danced and drank with joyful abandon. These clubs featured a "Who's who" list of Jazz greats : Duke Ellington, Errol Garner, Miles Davis, Charlie Parker, Max Roach... The audience was also part of the show. The best known among the regular crowd were philosopher Jean-Paul Sartre, father figure of the philosophy

soon known as existentialism — writers Albert Camus and Richard Wright and singer Juliette Greco.

In his *Manual for Saint-Germain*, Vian wrote, "Every night, fashion designers, models, 50 or 60 photographers, journalists, students, musicians, Americans, Swedes, English, Brazilians. It was a court of miracles or a tower of Babel, your choice..." The climate was, "a little bit like that of the sixth arrondissement but it's a little different and that difference makes all the difference. The temperature isn't much higher but the air is invigorating and better for your health. It sometimes rains in Saint-Germain-des-Prés, but only on those who do not live there..." A number of African-Americans had also chosen to live in Paris. Richard Wright, whose *Native Son*, broke new ground for African-American literature, settled there in 1947. Chester Himes wrote many detective novels in Paris, among them, *Cotton Comes to Harlem*. Drummer Kenny Clarke also chose to live in Paris. But the most famous of all jazz expatriates was doubtless Sidney Bechet, who made France his second home in 1949. And the French made his *Petite Fleur* a legendary all-time hit. ∎

All the great jazz stars performed in Paris after the Liberation. Like Louis Armstrong (opposite, top) or Duke Ellington (opposite, below with Boris Vian and Juliette Gréco). Others, like Kenny Clarke and Sidney Bechet (above with Errol Garner) made France their second home.

Right : *Miles Davis and Jeanne Moreau during the filming of* Elevator for the Scaffold.

Yesterday, Today and Tomorrow

Every friendship has its turbulent moments. Antoine de Saint-Exupéry, who knew the complexities of human nature, realized that even hearty friendships forged on a battlefield, could also be bruised and sometimes fractured. In a letter, written shortly before his death in 1945, and never revised, Saint-Exupéry speaks to this subject as timely now as it was 50 years ago :

"American friends : We must be fair to you. Someday, disputes of one kind or another may come between us. Every nation is egotistic. Every nation considers its egotism sacred. One day the fact of your material wealth will give you advantages that we consider unjust. At some point, we may have arguments that are more or less serious. If wars are always won by the idealists, peace treaties are usually written by the businessmen. So if one day, I find myself strongly opposed to the decisions of those men, I will never forget that, in this War, your aims were noble... It was not for gold that the mothers of America gave their sons in battle; nor did those young men accept that fate for financial gain. I have realized this and later on I will, in my own country, bear witness to the passion and faith with which each and every one of you committed yourselves to those ideals."

Antoine de Saint-Exupéry

ACKNOWLEDGMENTS

The publisher would like to thank those who helped make this book possible, especially : Mr. Marc Finaud, Assistant Director of Information at the French Ministry of Foreign Affairs; Mr. Michel Fabre, director of the Center for Afro-American Studies and Professor Emeritus at the Sorbonne, who shared with us the benefit of his extensive knowledge as well as his archives ; Lynn Weiss, assistant professor of English and American Literature at Washington University, who carefully revised the American version ; Mr. Jean-Pierre Daubresse, whose vast resources on Jazz were most valuable ; and all those who worked so enthusiastically on this project.

PHOTO CREDITS

Cover : Keystone. Inset La Fayette : Giraudon. P.1 : Jean-Loup Charmet. P. 2 ,3, 4, 5 : National Archives. P. 6 et 7 : Roger Viollet. P. 8 et 9 : R.M.N.. P. 10 : Jean-Loup Charmet. P.11 : Giraudon. P. 11-12 : Dite/IPS (La Fayette et Washington). P.12 : Tallandier (H) ; RMN (B). P. 13 : Jean-Loup Charmet. P. 14 et 15 : B.N.. P. 16 : Roger Viollet. P. 17 : Tallandier. P. 18 : Jean-Loup Charmet. P. 18-19 : RMN. P. 19 : Musée de Bérancourt. P. 20 : B.N.. P. 21 : Giraudon. P. 22 : Roger Viollet. P. 23 : MNHN Paris. P. 24 : Hulton Deutsch (G) ; Cinémagence/Paramount (D). P. 25 : D.R. (H) ; Hulton Deutsch (B). P. 26 : Jean-Loup Charmet. P. 27 : Musée Carnavalet. P. 28 : Giraudon (H) ; D.R. (B). P. 29 : D.R.. P. 30 et 31 : F. Flameng/Jean-Loup Charmet. P. 32 : L'Illustration/Sygma. P. 33 : Tallandier. P. 34 : Hulton Deutsch. P. 35 : L'Illustration/Sygma. P. 36 : J.-P. Gillet (H) ; dessin Ray Hutchins (B). P. 37 : Léon Hornecker/ L'Illustration. P. 38 : USIS/Tallandier (H) ; L'Illustration/Sygma (B). P. 39 : USIS/Tallandier. P. 40 : L'Illustration/Sygma. P. 41 : Keystone. P. 42 : D.R.. P. 43 : Keystone/Sygma. P. 44 : Col. Yacht Club de France/Jean-Loup Charmet. P. 45 : Jean-Loup Charmet. P. 46 : Keystone. P. 47 : Keystone (H) ; B : Roger Viollet (B). P. 48-49 : Keystone. P. 49 : L'Illustration/Sygma (H) ; Keystone (B). P. 50 et 51 : Keystone. P. 52 et 53 : Centre Culturel américain (H, D) ; National Archives (autres). P. 54 : National Archives. P. 56 : US Army/Tallandier. P. 57 : National Archives. P. 58 : Keystone. P. 59 : Tallandier. P. 60 : Keystone. P. 61 : Tallandier. P. 62 et 63 : Keystone. P. 64 : Jean-Loup Charmet.